ALSO BY FRANK BIDART

Golden State

The Book of the Body

The Sacrifice

In the Western Night: Collected Poems 1965–1990

Desire

Star Dust

Watching the Spring Festival

Metaphysical Dog

Half-light: Collected Poems 1965–2016

AS EDITOR

The Collected Poems of Robert Lowell (with David Gewanter)

AGAINST SILENCE

AGAINST SILENCE

FRANK BIDART

FARRAR STRAUS GIROUX

NEW YORK

Farrar, Straus and Giroux
120 Broadway, New York 10271

Copyright © 2021 by Frank Bidart
All rights reserved
Printed in the United States of America
First edition, 2021

Library of Congress Cataloging-in-Publication Data
Names: Bidart, Frank, 1939– author.
Title: Against silence / Frank Bidart.
Description: First edition. | New York : Farrar, Straus and Giroux, 2021.
Identifiers: LCCN 2021015864 | ISBN 9780374603519 (hardcover)
Subjects: LCGFT: Poetry.
Classification: LCC PS3552.I33 A72 2021 | DDC 811/.54—dc23
LC record available at https://lccn.loc.gov/2021015864

Our books may be purchased in bulk for promotional,
educational, or business use. Please contact your local
bookseller or the Macmillan Corporate and Premium
Sales Department at 1-800-221-7945, extension 5442, or by
email at MacmillanSpecialMarkets@macmillan.com.

www.fsgbooks.com
www.twitter.com/fsgbooks
www.facebook.com/fsgbooks

10 9 8 7 6 5 4 3 2 1

CONTENTS

PART ONE

Why the Dead Cannot Answer

A light, just now living, that has
never been, in its mortal life, turned off—

ON, it has never been, in its mortal
life, not ON,—

... when you ask what it is like

suddenly for what was always there
not to be there

for what had to be endured by those before you
to have to be endured now by you

LIKE, what in the world are such pervasive
vanishings LIKE,—

... no words it knows apply, and it is silent.

Silent. This is "the eternal silence of the dead."

At the Shore

All over the earth,
elegies for the earth.

The shore is in mourning. It mourns what it must soon

see, the sea
rising—

implacable, drowning chunks of the intelligible, familiar world.

Creatures of the earth filled with the instinct to wound
the earth. We fear that by an act of immense, unconscious

will, we have succeeded at last in killing NATURE.

Since childhood, you hated the illusion that this
green and pleasant land

inherently is green
or pleasant

or for human beings home. Whoever dreamed that had

not, you thought, experienced
the earth. *We needed to rewrite in revenge the world that wrote us.*

•

My parents drove from the Sierras (Bishop), to the almost-
city of their parents, carved from desert (Bakersfield).

To get anywhere you had to cross the Mojave Desert.

It was World War Two. In the Sierras my father was a big shot.
He said *It's better to be a big fish in a little pond.* The government

didn't draft—even

refused to enlist—rich
farmers. So to my mother's dismay, night after night in bars

drunk, wronged, he fought soldiers who had called him a coward.

They drove their gorgeous Lincoln Zephyr across the steaming
    Mojave at night.
Half-

carsick, I was in the back seat, inside,
protected.

Unprotected. Phantasmagoric enormous

tumbleweeds in the empty
landscape rolled aimlessly outside the speeding car.

Mourning What We Thought We Were

We were born into an amazing experiment.

At least we thought we were. We knew there was no
escaping human nature: my grandmother

taught me that: my own pitiless nature
taught me that: but we exist inside an order, I

thought, of which history
is the mere shadow—

  •

Every serious work of art about America has the same
theme: *America*

is a great IDEA: the reality leaves something to be desired.

Bakersfield. Marian Anderson, the first great black classical
contralto, whom the Daughters of the American Revolution

would not allow to sing in an unsegregated

Constitution Hall, who then was asked by Eleanor
Roosevelt to sing before thousands at the Lincoln Memorial

was later refused a room at the Padre Hotel, Bakersfield.

My mother's disgust
as she told me this. It confirmed her judgment about

what she never could escape, where she lived out her life.

My grandmother's fury when, at the age of seven or
eight, I had eaten at the home of a black friend.

The forced camps at the end of *The Grapes of Wrath*

were outside
Bakersfield. When I was a kid, *Okie*

was still a common term of casual derision and contempt.

•

So it was up to us, born
in Bakersfield, to carve a new history

of which history is the mere shadow—

•

To further the history of the S P I R I T is our work,—

. . . therefore thank you, Lord
Whose Bounty Proceeds by Paradox,

for showing us we have failed to change.

•

Dark night, December 1st 2016.

White supremacists, once again in
America, are acceptable, respectable. America!

Bakersfield was first swamp, then
desert. We are sons of the desert
who cultivate the top half-inch of soil.

Words Reek Worlds

1

Dreaming, I dreamt the basket I held held
words. Words that are the thousand flowers of
fury, *ressentiment*, words stunted by relentless
schisms within myself, too little intention, too much—

I fiercely clung to them, as the only words I had.

Dreaming, I saw a woman swaddling
something.

She wailed and said, "Blind."

2 A Voice You Recognize Explains the Term "Running a Train"

Rich boys who got a leash dug deep into their
necks pay to watch what
they can't do at home. *Running a train? You find a badass,*
    dumbass
hood-rat that loves
cock, then ten guys pass the cunt

slowly around like a blunt. The old guys don't like that there are cameras
everywhere, but they—like
everybody else—
want to see.
The young guys have been preparing for this since
childhood,
but are amazed
it's happening. Or almost happening. Just
don't get my face and dick in the same frame.

3

There is an abyss there. *There*
is an abyss there. In the flat,

unfamiliar
ordinary, you hear an abyss.

Advice-giver, take your own advice.

Set up a situation,—
. . . then reveal an abyss.

4

Words, voices reek of the worlds from which they
emerge: different worlds, each with its all but palpable
aroma, its parameters, limitations, promise.

Words—there is a gap, nonetheless always
and forever, between words and the world—

slip, slide, are imprecise, BLIND, perish.

At times, when you are lucky, someone who isn't
lying talks.

What you believe is what is for the speaker
unchosen, where, after
stumbling, someone fell.

When you believe what you hear, what you believe is a voice.

5

Between the voice that says *Rich boys*
pay to watch what they can't do at home

and what, for that voice, then follows

is an abyss,—the abyss is

meaning. Not
has meaning.

You've read *The Chinese Written Character As
a Medium for Poetry. Eisenstein On Montage.*

It is a new (slight) object in the world. Is.

6

You can turn it and turn it
in the light. Why have I given the reader this

smart but ruthless, resourceful
entrepreneur

who wants not only to entertain but
shock us? The words

are everything and

nothing. You turn and turn them
in the light. There is a new object in the world.

7

Absurd. You are trying to rescue poetry, WORDS, art itself, all
    these chiseled
lurches.

8   Images—Words Aspiring To Be Without Voice

Two guys alone in a car in a huge
parking lot that is empty. The car
is a few feet from the concrete
wall that bounds the lot as far as the camera can see.
The car is large, comfortable. The boys, high, are
jousting familiarly
about which of them, in King Arthur's court, would be
king. You can tell they have had this argument before.
White suburban middle-class kids
smoking, drinking, wasting time on a warm fall night.

Then the driver starts the car. We hear him yell in
exhilaration as he
rams the large car into the concrete wall.

Thus begins Gia Coppola's
film of James Franco's *Palo Alto*.

9

As you arm yourself, as you go out among the tribe of makers in
words—arm yourself with phrases,

Set up a situation,—
. . . then reveal an abyss.

Duende.   Sprung Rhythm.

Or (my favorite, paraphrased from Yeats)

Out of our argument with others we make
rhetoric, out of our argument with ourselves we make poetry—

As I swagger out, armed (as I think) with
the secret of representation, as I swagger out among the tribes

I become aware that I am armed with a pebble against the ocean,
     though
I speak I am silent.

10   (Made in Africa)

LORD GOD OF ARMIES, you
who is the macrocosm, I

entrust you to the end my physical
BODY, my mental
BODY, and my psychic
BODY

finally that your holy trinity
is fulfilled in my expiatory kingdom.

(Noah Yannick Joseph, December 28, 2018, 7:46AM,
Sousseri, Cameroon: Facebook)

We share aesthetic predilections. Each old thing

new-made, home
made.

Fucked over by the old lies, the old
words must be remade to tell the truth.

The Moral Arc of the Universe Bends Toward Justice

is an illusion. *It's true, it's human nature to try to*
unbend

what for centuries human nature—with great wisdom, great
pain—bent.

What had to be built we knew instinctively must be built
without

asking permission of the ignorant doing the building. But natural
pity

soon ends
when what pity unleashes is CHAOS, is

horror.
The cauldron that has always been the source

of force
we have learnt slowly, in time, how to control. Have learnt to

enslave
(you would harshly say) more subtly. More, you would say, cunningly.

Think the American Civil War,—
. . . followed by a century of Jim Crow.

If you do not become a master
you are a slave.

     •

The voice of *What had to be built* leaves certain
words bodiless. The Lost Cause, strange

fruit, was lost, for us, in a song about lacerated flesh.

When a master stares at himself in the future

what he fears is that the world will do to him what
he did to the world when he was the world.

Behind the Lion

(SIDNEY BECHET—HIS WORDS)

I order up a couple of gins, and when they're
brought to us, I put

this coin on the table, this half-crown.

And there's this king's
picture on it, like a snapshot.

It was a funny thing looking at your
money and seeing somebody you'd know.

I could still
see him sitting there
tapping his feet.

•

There was over a thousand people there.

It was the first time I got to
recognize somebody
from having seen his picture on my money.

•

We had the whole
royal family
tapping their feet.

·

There were no
charges against me. But

the judge who was doing the case,—
. . . he wouldn't

clear the deportation charge.

·

A coin. That's something with
two sides

and I'd seen
both of them.

You put a lion in back of a king,—
. . . and that's a big thing.

But you look
BEHIND the lion,—
                    (*IF* you could look
behind the lion,—)

there's nothing to see but cops.

●

—That half-crown, it's too much of a tip
for two gins. I just leave it

there on the table.

When I'm on the boat, I look for all the English
money I've got, all the C O I N S, and chuck them overboard.

The Fifth Hour of the Night

The sun allows you to see only what the sun
falls
upon: the surface. What we wanted was what was elsewhere: cause.

    •

Or some books say that's what we once wanted. Prophets of
cause
never, of course, agreed about cause, the *uncaused* Cause: or they

    •

terribly did. Asleep, I struggle to stay inside sleep, unravaged by
heart-
piercing dreams—craving, wish, desire to remain inside, if briefly,

    •

obliteration. I cleave to the voice of Poppea's nurse:
oblivion
soave.

    •

Not frightening, the word
oblivion
as Oralia Dominguez, hauntingly clinging to the sound, in 1964
    sings it.

II

Eating today, however
satisfying, frees no creature from having to eat tomorrow. *Sun*

cycle
built into us. It's because you are an animal with a body.

However
filling.

As soon as adolescent sex ended this hunger
that you had not known was yours until the moment you

satisfied it, at the moment you satisfied it
the hunger returned.

It would never be satisfied. It would
never not return.

Cycle
built into us, returning each day like the sun's diurnal

round: in adolescence, more than once each
round. It's because you are an animal with a body.

•

The night we found we were starving, what
larks! With what

relish we devoured dish upon dish placed in front of us.

-

Cycle of the sun that each day.

Cycle of the sun that each day wipes the slate.

Promises to wipe the slate.

Deep wrongness between the two that somehow nothing can wipe
    clean.

They love each other more than anything and their child knows
    that.

They love each other more than anything but the well is poisoned.

Thirst no well can satisfy.

The well of affection that bloods the house is poisoned.

Love that bloods the house is poisoned.

He was smart and good-looking and charmed everyone.

She was beautiful and smart and charmed everyone.

Deep wrongness between the two that somehow no fury can wipe
    clean.

Thirst no wife and child can slake or satisfy.

The well is poisoned.

The well that allows you to think the earth your hand touches is good.

•

Gone, except within anyone who had lived there.

•

Unforgotten hour. Permanent
horizon-line

you cannot rip from your eye. Permanent
under-taste

you cannot
untaste. *Hour that stains, unerasable, unforgotten.*

III

Sun that, each day, promises. Cycle of the sun that each day
reconciles
creatures that flinch at pain, sentience reconciled to the predations of

•

ordinary existence. After food, after
satiation,
shit. Poppea? We know her name because she risked becoming

•

Empress. Nero, who made her, as she wanted, Empress, later
kicked
her to death. She had few, had no illusions about what would

•

follow getting what she wanted. Monteverdi's ruthless
librettist
imagines a Poppea who believes in nothing—and tries everything.

•

After one, exhausted by the attempt, has tasted each thing the sun
offers,
erasure

•

more than half-
desired.
What is too little, mysteriously tips into . . . too much. Surfeit

·

breeds loathing. *Oh sun-worshippers, sun-*
treaders:—
creatures

·

endowed with what they have learned are mouths and teeth
dream
not repetition, ease of unendingly getting whatever you must eat, but

·

sudden
vision,—
after twisting fogbound dizzying hairpin mountain turns in darkness for

·

hours, the vehicle in which you are riding, are TRAPPED, is abruptly
above
the clouds, you

·

see, for the first time, the ancient
GLACIER
whose gigantic face rises past sleeping farmhouses in eerily calm
moonlight.

•

In 1961, at the Simplon Pass, a remnant of the Ice Age
thrust
upon me the sublime. Now it is melting. I read that it is melting, for

•

miles has melted. By the child's fifth year, the poisoned house was
gone,
except within anyone who had lived there. The crack that replaced it

•

went down and down, went through everything
bottomlessly.
I thought it had to have an end but could see no end. Or the crack

•

was not a crack, but an invisible
indivisible
living seam—joining love and hate

•

seamlessly, *this* and what seemed *not-this*
savagely
suddenly melting into each other.

  •

It was the sun-filled, seamless surface of glare-filled
reality,
full of cracks. I was trapped in a small dark house, my grandmother's

  •

house, full of cracks. After the divorce, my grandmother and I
loved
watching wrestling together, lost before the screen of our first TV.

  •

One day I told her (I must have been
seven,
eight) that, after school that afternoon, I had eaten

  •

at the house of a new friend. The family lived
two
blocks away. They were black.

  •

Fury. Her sudden fury made
clear
that as long as I lived in her house, I must not

     .

enter or eat at his house again. Must
not
remain his friend.

     .

The rage I felt at what she demanded did not
preclude
my furious but supine eventual acquiescence.

     .

I was a coward. *I was a coward.* I never
forgave
her. I never forgave her for showing

     .

me
me.
For years I drew thousands of floorplans for the perfect

     .

house, but what remained unerasable, without solution were
her
and me. Small dark labyrinthine

•

house without end. One day I swung at her. The half-door window I smashed
cut my wrist close to the artery. I did not wish her

•

her death. What did she see outside the open third-floor hospital window
one night from her room she climbed into?—

•

For years, his half-expectant, then
indifferent
eyes as I walked past. I told myself we had nothing in common. He
was a jock.

•

In the years that followed, impossible to heal
what my coward hand had severed.

•

After centuries, at last my father's only son, the maw more and more ravenous
within him, discovered that what he could

•

make (the mania somehow was to
make,
he discovered that he must make—) was

.

poetry. Dark anti-matter matter whose matter is
words
in which the seam and the crack (*what Emerson*

.

called the crack in everything God made) are in
fury
fused, annealed, ONE.

IV

His circumspection hides, but does not quite hide, thirst too-like his
    father's.
His mother's constant admonishment that what he must not be is
    his father.
What as a kid I loathed in my father, now I understand.
Aging men want to live inside sharp desire again before they die.
The terrible law of desire is that what quickens desire is what is
    DIFFERENT.
Thirst for the mirror on which is written: *Fuck me like the whore I am.*
Thirst for erasing the pretense of love.

Thirst for the end of endless negotiation.
Thirst for the glamour and magic that cost too much.
Thirst, hidden but not quite hidden, for buying submission to your
    will.
They will see that what you have bought is compliance.
Thirst for fuck the cost.

.

No one formula for the incompatibilities that
are
existence.

.

Sleeping in a motel with my father, when he, in anguish and crying,
implored
me to try to get my mother to return to him,

.

I said I
would,—
. . . and knew I wouldn't.

.

At the bottom of existence, contradictory necessary
demands
unsolvable, a dilemma.

.

Both my parents ended their lives—lives as flesh—seemingly
without
catharsis. Amid trivia and resentment and incompletion, the end.

        •

My mother's anguish at walls onto which, as a child, I had flung
shit.
No scrubbing can clean them. If, somewhere in death, my mother

        •

has her will, she is still scrubbing. Again and again now I return to
drink
from the poisoned well, but she cannot see this. Ineradicable

        •

disgust at
existence
that, to my terror, intermittently rises in me, she

        •

senses—but cannot name. She is bewildered by such
anger
in her child. She wonders when, tonight, he will sleep, what

        •

he will in time love. Now, she sees that he is
writing,
writing. She is afraid of what he writes: *Sun-worshipper,*

.

your fellow sun-treaders
run
the world. Watch as they kneel to the sun.

PART TWO

The Ghost

You must not think that what I have
accomplished through you

could have been accomplished by any other means.

Each of us is to himself
indelible. I had to become that which could not

be, by time, from human memory, erased.

I had to burn my hungry, unappeasable
furious spirit

so inconsolably into you

you would without cease
write to bring me rest.

Bring us rest. Guilt is fecund. I knew

nothing I made
myself had enough steel in it to survive.

I tried: I made beautiful
paintings, beautiful poems. Fluff. Garbage.

The inextricability of love and hate?

If I had merely made you
love me you could not have saved me.

Poem with a Refrain from LeRoy Chatfield

Last night after midnight, or would that be today? unable to sleep,

I watched movies to remind myself
about our nature.

You feel less woe that we do not change when you watch
movies about our nature.

Ambition. Jealousy. Unacknowledged

paranoia, unacknowledged
addiction. The screenwriter who cannot sell a screenplay

latches on to the rich ex-movie-goddess
dreaming of a comeback. He is doing it only until he

can get on his feet. Or the ex-movie-star
who has guided the career of his young protégé

perfectly and can in his own case see his own future
perfectly

so we watch him walk into the sea. Why he does what he does

is, in some sense, clear, though how to deflect
any of it, deflect his death and fate

is opaque. He is familiar
and opaque.

The restored yet forever still-
butchered Garland A *Star Is Born*

reminds me that what, at fifteen, in 1954, I could not
persuade my mother and step-father to drive

a hundred and twelve miles from Bakersfield to Hollywood
to see

in my lifetime I
cannot ever see.

Last night after midnight, or would that be today? unable to sleep.

The Great, the One Subject

. . . how the world we find ourselves in
happened. *(Each*

world we find ourselves in
that is, for us, the world.)

                  I've gone from being the only

member of my cohort whose mother had
died, to everyone's mother is dead.

Lloyd, Peg, Robert, Louise, David.

From being the only member of my cohort both of whose
parents are dead, to (unperceived, imperceptible

because incremental, as if
random)
            one day you see the parents of every body your age

are. The last layer, final
buffer between us and the cuisinart breath of the universe

wiped away. Disappeared, they have been disappeared. A world.

•

Just when you thought the superhighway would
get you there, it

ends, it dumps you onto two-lane twisty country roads.

You had been seized by the desire to reach the end. Now
you are surrounded, as so

often, by clutter
intricate, familiar.

Who knows how long this will go on?—

•

She had made a mistake. The same error
over and over. Not

over and over: TWICE. The second
was meant to correct the first.

It did not correct the first. It turns out

the opposite of what you hate
you can also grow to hate.

It cannot be made right, not when
she has made it not once but twice.

·

He clung to his anger. It is his shield
against her. All she asked

was that her son forgive her. Whatever

dictatorial cruelty
she had been driven to, was because

her son was surrounded by wolves—
including his father. Which he is

too young
not to be blind to. Why can't he

forgive her—? He

cannot. Another story of
a house where

blind the blind are driven.

·

He cannot. She thinks forgiveness is
erasing the past, *tabula*

rasa. Leaving him without
memory, without his only

weapon. She would make him
a lapdog. He

cannot. As if the famous injunction to
forgive

were ruthless, her stratagem.

.

Then she died. He did
not die. Her house that she made and despised

folded up, and moved
inside him. The world

he grew up in
which already lived inside him

and was infinite

grew finite, mere memory. She learned in
death that once you are dead, as when

alive, it's hard to change the past.

·

What do committees do, he thought, *except decide who gets sacrificed.*

Never
enough. Money, the places that are available

are never
enough. Choices, therefore,

must be made. *Something over-vehement, something relished, punitive, insufficiently*

skeptical, about the decisions made by every committee you've ever been on. Something

enjoyed. You get to decide who doesn't get any.

He hated the faintly smug, self-satisfied deployments of power. He had learned how

to charm
early. Others didn't. He knew instinctively.

·

He craved the superhighway. He had spent
enough time in the dirt

subtly moving dirt around. He was
tired seeing nothing.

Poem Beginning With Words by Lisel Mueller

There are two of us here. Then, *Touch me.*
The words

make me want never to be touched again.

The person you desire to touch but
who does not desire you

Who does not want to investigate your body

did not choose what he desires
just as you did not choose what you desire.

That does not make his rejection, his recoil

and indifference, any less
feel like judgment. I like the word

prowler. They that prowl

prowl for what they do not
possess.

You are what I do not possess. I mean

you allow me to touch you
but you do not want to be touched.

As I lay

half-asleep today, half-
dreaming, you said to me matter-of-factly

I want you to move out of my apartment—

though (you say smiling) you must
continue paying the rent. At this, I woke.

You appeared as a woman, but I saw through that.

Since adolescence, I saw that what cannot be
possessed generates

lust—

(secretly, how relieved we are to find, yet again, for
each of us, what generates

lust—). I tell you, angrily: *What one creature*

lacks, its lover
is trained by that lack, again and then again, to covet.

Then I hear your voice, slowly, brokenly:

Sadness, GUILT, keeping all your feelings
stuffed down inside

while friends try to pry it all out of you—

what you accuse me of is right. It's half my
charm, my sweet spot ... How are you doing?

Are you taking care of yourself?

Love's ruined, melancholy
spectacle. My wanting too much from him

was driven by as much

necessity as his
inability to give more. Since adolescence, I

refused to play,—

... in time, we meet someone with whom we
cannot (thirst

without bottom) with whom we cannot

whatever our will
refuse to play. This is the universal law of love

love & sex & desire

balanced, perfectly
universally

unbalanced.

Teach me. When you
want me, I don't think this is true. When you don't, I do.

Dialogue With Flesh

It was all a dialogue with flesh. Every

moment. Dialogue
with what you were not. Were

and were not—were not
flesh, and were. I blamed

my mother and grandmother and father

as if they were
souls, not flesh—

vowed never to have a child

(at seven or eight, solemnly vowed
never to make a creature like me) because no

creature must ever
conceivably feel about

me what I felt about him.

•

Vowed to cut myself away from
what clearly even then I knew were the common

patterns governing human life—

furious love, followed by
furious hatred.

Two people in a room. Then three.

  •

With what you were, and were
not. Dialogue

every moment. With flesh, and not.

Coda

(NEITHER MASTER / NOR SLAVE)

When this body that we find ourselves in at birth at last
dies,

    and what we have hoped (hoped at
best—) is past death to rejoin the vast silence that precedes birth

   •

You see the hand
before you that you think is

your hand
and there by your decision

is a chimera
you cast on a smooth crowded impenetrable mirror wall that you

face, chimera

cast by the immense
bright light behind you that you cannot turn your head to see.

   •

When this body begins to wear out, die
like anything

else that blossoms, withers, and dies

	•

All our lives we have heard and reheard words of con-men
and tortured
visionaries prophesying

what must happen when the body that you find yourself

	•

in at birth

	•

the gnarled, old hand
that one day you look down and see

one day you see is yours

	II

Mind at war with its ground.

	•

Think of the earth—matter, the mind's
ground—as an enormous mirror

across whose impenetrable surface the individual
soul fears that it merely appears and disappears

without weight, another among multitudinous
chimera, without identity or consequence.

Dispensable. Without identity or
force, erased among numberless infinities.

One finger

reached out toward the wall across
whose surface you are

a chimera

and with its one knife-like
nail

deep as you could

dug into it. Almost in
delirium, you scratched the screen with a jagged scratch.

•

Before it happened,
it was never going to happen.

After it happened,
it was always going to happen.

    •

Not the deepest scratch. In
triumph, you were almost indifferent to how deep,—

. . . but deep.

    •

Mind returns the intolerable in art / as brilliant dream.

On My Seventy-Eighth

There will be just two at
table tonight,
though to accommodate all those who have
so mattered
and still so matter in my life, the table will be
very long:
though empty. I say to you, *Jaya*
shoma khalee!
Your place is empty! Your place at my table
is saved
for you. I tried to construct in my soul
your necessary
grave (because you were dead/because you were
flawed/preoccupied,
concentrated on your soul, too often you were
cruel—) but
as I shoveled dirt onto your body, the dirt refused,
soon, to
cling. Those who torment because you know you
loved them
refuse to remain buried. *Is anything ever forgotten,*
actually forgiven?
Shovel in hand, I saw how little I had
known you.

Tonight, I abjure the wisdom, the illusion of
forgetting. Come,
give up silence. Intolerable the fiction
the rest
is silence. To the dead, to the living:
your place
is empty.

Acknowledgments

All the words of "Behind the Lion" are from Sidney Bechet's autobiography, *Treat It Gentle* (Hill and Wang, 1960). One dinner with Kaveh Akbar gave me the Farsi of "On My Seventy-Eighth."

The poems in this book first appeared, often in somewhat different form, in the following publications: *Freeman's California* (Grove Press, 2019), *Literary Imagination, Literary Hub, The New Yorker, Poem-a-Day, The Pushcart Prize XLV: Best of the Small Presses* (W. W. Norton & Co., 2021), *The Paris Review, Salmagundi,* and *The Threepenny Review.*